"Keep doing the work you are doing Georgina. It's very precious."
- Thomas Moore, *Care of the Soul*

"This book is a little gem."
- Kerry

"Georgina is genuinely gifted and in a deep integral connection with nature and all her beings. Her healing energy shines through."
- Mhairead

"Georgina takes you on a journey where death re-finds its natural place alongside birth and life. She offers a deeply honest, helpful and healing approach to living well and dying well."
- Rebecca

"Your wisdom and your strength was a portal for me to be able to see my own."
- Emily

"A plant alchemist, apothecary and shaman with deep wisdom and true healing gifts."
- Stefania

"You reminded me that I am a little bit magic, that we all are."
- Kristin

"The way you have cared for family and friends at the end of life by gently linking them to nature, has been profound. As a nurse I have seen just how special it is for everyone in the room."
- Olivia

"Working with Georgina was an absolute joy. I learned techniques from her that aided me as I navigated doctors' appointments and surgeries."
- Gretchen

"Georgina led me on a beautiful journey that left me feeling inspired, on purpose, and powerful."
- Brenna

50 THINGS TO HELP WHEN
LIFE CHANGES

For Sam

50 THINGS TO HELP WHEN LIFE CHANGES

Contemplative and Nature-based Teachings for Navigating Life Transitions

GEORGINA LANGDALE

Archeus Publishing

Archeus Publishing
PO Box 8759
Havelock North 4130
New Zealand

Copyright © 2024 by Georgina Langdale

All rights reserved. No part of this book may be reproduced in any manner whatsoever without written permission except in the case of brief quotations embodied in critical articles and reviews.

No part of this book may be reproduced in any form or by any means, electronic or mechanical, including photography, recording, or by any information storage and retrieval system or technologies now known or later developed, without permission in writing from the publisher.

ISBN 978-0-473-70258-8

Interior photographs by Georgina Langdale

First Printing, 2024

Contents

Introduction		1
Rose Poem		3
1	Rest in the Space Between Breaths	6
2	Silver Birch is a Deep Protective Spirit	8
3	The Wisdom of 'Don't Know' Mind	10
4	Speaking from the 'I'	12
5	What the Seasons can Teach Us	14
6	The Soothing Power of Tonglen	16
7	Peace and Gratitude	18
8	The Gift of Open Questions	20
9	The Threads that Join Us Together	22
10	The Balance of Oak	24
11	Working with the Flow of the Stream	26
12	Being in the Moment	28
13	Finding a Safe Place to Land in the Middle of Things	30
14	Tapping to Help Relieve Anxiety	32

15	Breathing into Pain	34
16	What Really Matters	36
17	Helping Those You Love Care for You	38
18	Paperwork for Peace of Mind	40
19	Finding a Place to Meet (even when absent)	42
20	Transformational Power of an Altar	44
21	Aromatics as Medicine for The Soul	46
22	The Asclepieion Temple of Dreams	48
23	Being the Tree	50
24	Images as Amulets	52
25	Communication Counts	54
26	Look Deep into Nature	56
27	The Empty Vessel	58
28	The Power of Thought	60
29	Counting Breaths I	62
30	Meeting People Where They Are	64
31	Writing Letters for the Future	66
32	Finding Your Spirit Animal	68
33	Working with the Moon	70
34	The Power of Plant Essences	72
35	The Power of Ceremony	74
36	Counting Breath II	76

37	Handing Back the Wounds that are Not Yours to Carry	78
38	A Blessing for Your Body	80
39	Holding Healing Space	82
40	Talking to Children	84
41	Speaking Silently Through the Heart	86
42	I Am Still Standing	88
43	Bringing Nature into the Room	90
44	Creating Guided Visualisations	92
45	Everything is Energy (how we show up for others)	94
46	Don't Be Afraid of Silence	96
47	Written in the Sky	98
48	Don't Hold Back, Experience Everything	100
49	Fire as a Tool for Transformation	102
50	In the End Love is All There Is	104

About the Author	107
Acknowledgments	109
Helpful Links & Information	111
Notes On Images	113
About Archeus Publishing	117

Introduction

I believe that when our approach to navigating life embraces emotional, physical and spiritual needs, great transformation can occur, and my hope is that you will find ideas in this book that can support you on your own transformational journey.

This book is about finding things to help when life changes. The end of a relationship, death, illness, financial or employment loss are all events that can turn life as we know it upside down. Somewhere in all this we need to find ways to care for ourselves, build resilience, and care for others too. Maybe you have been supporting a loved one for some time. Perhaps you are now finding yourself supporting someone you love whose life has suddenly changed completely. Perhaps it is you who has been given a life-limiting prognosis. Maybe you are facing starting life all over again as a relationship ends. My hope is that this book will help you find a place of calm in the midst of things.

Over the past decade I have used these techniques in a range of different contexts; from the workplace, talking to a stranger on the phone, being at the bedside in a hospice, sharing techniques with friends wanting to help a friend, helping the newly divorced woman figure out how to get her life back on track, creating blessings for the dead, comforting the bereaved, supporting someone as they start arduous medical treatment, being there for them when the doctor says, "see you in three months", and in navigating my own transitions.

I have created this book as something that you can dip in and out of as you need to, swooping and diving like a bird on the wing, coming to land on things to help you and those you love.

Georgina Langdale

Rose Poem

The red rose flowers.
I tried to take it where
it did not want to go.
I tried to make it climb
but it wanted to be a bush.
Until one day I saw it
for who it was,
and set it free.
Now the rose flowers
abundantly.

Georgina Langdale

I

Rest in the Space Between Breaths

Managing our breath consciously is a key to managing our emotions.

If you are trying to find ways to calm down, focus on your breath. Breathe in and feel the spaciousness of the pause between the in-breath and the out-breath.

Do this for a few breaths and you will feel yourself growing calmer.

2

Silver Birch is a Deep Protective Spirit

There is a healing power in Nature that we can all tap into. Trees, plants, flowers, shrubs, herbs offer ways of managing our emotions and finding resilience when life changes. Each has its own character and life force that, once aware of, we can be drawn to connecting with to help give us extra support in our daily life.

The Silver Birch tree has deep mythological power and is said to have a deeply protective feminine energy. In the northern hemisphere she is often known as The Lady of the Woods.

When you need some deep feminine or maternal energy around you, picture a silver birch tree, or if you can be with one physically, even better.

Place your hands on the trunk of the tree and image its energy moving through your hands and enveloping you in loving protection. Feel its grace and translucent beauty wrapping itself around you and merging with your own sense of being.

What other trees are you drawn to? Picture their energy and explore how you can work with that too.

3

The Wisdom of 'Don't Know' Mind

It's OK to not have all the answers. Often, we want to help someone, or we are being given information about a situation, and we want to think that we know the answers, or that we know exactly what to do. But this approach can mean we miss out on fully understanding what is going on.

Learning to work with the practice of 'don't know mind' can change the depth and nature of any discussions you may have in any part of your life. Rather than assuming you know how someone is feeling and thinking, or that you have the answers to a situation, imagine you know absolutely nothing at all.

Then, gently ask questions of the person so that you can start to 'know their world'. This approach can help you ask curious questions, and it also gives room for the other to express themselves more fully.

4

Speaking from the 'I'

Sometimes, without even meaning it, the way we speak to another person can sound confrontational or judgmental.

Often in conversation, we might think we are speaking our thoughts, but what we are actually saying is *'you this, you that, or we...'*

This can sound like we are imposing our thoughts on another person or telling them what to do.

When life changes, conversations can often be difficult as emotions are running high and so in these times, it can be much gentler to 'speak from the I'. This means that you are saying *'I think, I see this as... etc.'*

By speaking your thoughts truly as yourself, in the *'I'*, it is much easier for the other person to hear and respond to your words. Tip: You could even preface what you are about to say by saying, "I'm speaking from the *'I'* here."

5

What the Seasons can Teach Us

Throughout time, physicians, mystics, and healers have said that Nature is the greatest teacher of all. They have seen the power of seeing oneself reflected in the seasons and rhythms of nature.

If we look at the seasons: spring, summer, autumn, winter; we see that there is a time of new beginnings, a time of growth, a time of harvest and a time of turning inward and decay. Noticing this cycle can help us ask the question: "What do I need to bring into being?" or "What can I let go of now to fall like a leaf from the tree?" or "What things have had their time?", "What are the seeds I could be planting in my own life?"

The seasons remind us that nothing is static. Everything changes and life is a series of circular transitions into new ways of being.

6

The Soothing Power of Tonglen

There are times when we want to help a loved one, or a community, or a pet, or even the world, but we feel helpless and don't know how. A compassionate offering, we can give them is a beautiful Buddhist practice called *Tonglen*, which is so simple and has a profound power to soothe and help.

Here's what to do:

Get yourself comfortable, quiet, still and grounded.

Take some slow, deep breaths. Feel the stillness within you.

Feel your feet anchored to the floor and that there's a cord running through you, from the crown of your head, that is connecting you to infinity, or you might visualise it as a golden cord of light.

Then picture the person or object of your compassion. Take a few breaths picturing them.

When they are really clear to you, imagine that as you breathe in, you are breathing in all their pain.

Then feel yourself releasing it to the universe.

As you breath out, imagine that you are filling them with loving kindness.

The trick to this is that you breathe in their pain, but you don't hold onto it. You release it, and then you breathe loving kindness into them. Breathing in their pain and breathing out loving kindness. A gentle cycle of compassion.

You can do this in the room with the person, or from half-way across the world. It doesn't matter which, it still works. You can even do it for someone in the past, or in the future. And for those moments when words are not found, this can be a beautiful practice to give.

7

Peace and Gratitude

Peace and gratitude are two words that are intimately interwoven. It is hard to have one without the other.

When times are difficult, developing a gratitude practice can help us find a place of peace within things. When waking up in the morning, think of three things to be grateful for. Then before going to sleep at night, take a moment to think of something that occurred during the day that you are grateful for. This simple practice can help bring balance to our emotions.

This beautiful call for peace is attributed to Celtic earth-based practices, and I also like to add this into my gratitude practice:

Deep within the still centre of my being
May I find peace.
Silently within the quiet of the Grove*
May I share peace.

*Gently within the greater circle of humankind
May I radiate peace.*

* The word *grove* means a group of trees with little undergrowth. Throughout time groves have been places for sacred ceremony.

8

The Gift of Open Questions

When life changes, we want to be able to understand what another person, often someone we love dearly, is thinking about what is happening.

Good conversation is made up of two types of questions, known as *open* and *closed* questions. If we only ask *closed* questions that just give the option of a yes or no answer, we will never fully understand, as the other person will not be able to truly express themselves.

Asking *open* questions creates an opportunity for true understanding and expression. For example, if someone asks you the *closed* question, "Do you like the colour blue?" You really only have the option to say yes, or no. But if they asked you an *open* question such as "What does the colour blue make you feel?" You are given the opportunity to say so much more.

Here are some more examples:

Closed question: Do you like dogs?
Open question: What does your dog make you think of?
Closed question: Are you looking forward to moving to your new home?
Open question: What opportunities do you think your move will give you?
Closed question: Are you scared about your treatment?
Open question: You are starting/ending some treatment. What are the things that bring you fear or anxiety at the moment?

When seeking to create space for someone to express themselves, try to use more *open* questions than *closed* ones. And also try to hold silence for them so they can have time to formulate their thoughts and answer.

These techniques will help enable is a key to you team up open questions with the wisdom of compassionate and transformational communication to take place.

9

The Threads that Join Us Together

I first learned of this beautiful way of deepening connection during a talk given by end-of-life doula, Gabby Jimenez, for the Conscious Dying Collective. In situations where a separation is going to occur, such as someone going away, or perhaps into hospital, this thread ceremony can help bring focus to the bonds between people. It is especially lovely to do with children.

Ideally it is good to get some different coloured embroidery threads or fine ribbons, one colour for each person. Cut each person a thread long enough to tie loosely around the recipient's wrist.

Imagine a family with four children and two adults. One of the parents, let's say the mother, is going into hospital. You would need six colours of thread. The mother takes a thread for each of their family and goes somewhere in the house or garden where each person can talk to them privately. Then one by one they call a member of their family to them and share something special that they want to say to them. Then they tie the thread around the child or partner's wrist. Part of this private sharing is to tell the child that each time they look at or touch the thread, the words will come back to them. At the end of this part of the ceremony, everyone will have a thread from the mother on their wrist.

For the next step, when that is done, the family members take their colour threads and one by one go to the mother, tell her something special and then tie the thread around her wrist as a reminder of their love. When this is done, everyone will have at least one thread around their wrist and all the words of love and support that were shared between them.

There is such tenderness in this ceremony, and for children it helps them feel that they are directly able to care and help their parent (in this example, the mother), and also feel the parent's love for them every time they touch their thread around their wrist.

10

The Balance of Oak

The Oak has always been seen as a sacred tree of strength and protection. Where the Silver Birch (No.2) is regarded as a feminine spirit, the oak is masculine.

I love working with oak as a protective energy for someone, but the magic goes even deeper. An oak's roots descend into the earth as deeply as its branches reach up into the sky. When you stand at the base of an oak tree, you are standing at a point of perfect balance.

If you are seeking the ability to be strong for others, but deep down you are tired and feeling out of balance, in being with oak and tuning in to its energy, which can be as simple as placing your hands on its trunk, leaning against it or sitting at its base, you are also tapping into its perfect balance.

If you are not able to be with an oak tree in nature, find an image of oak that you like and focus on it, place your hands on it and imagine drawing in its strength and balance.

11

Working with the Flow of the Stream

Water can cleanse us literally when we wash, but also metaphysically when we have emotions, events or memories we wish to release, or things we wish to bring in.

Working with the flow of a stream or river is a way of helping with the letting go and bringing in of things. To explain this idea I will tell a story of my own.

On the 7th anniversary of my mother's death, I returned to where I had buried her ashes, under a willow by a beautiful stream on our old farm. The stream was shallow and gentle and after some quiet meditation I stepped into the ankle-deep stream and faced downstream.

I spent some time feeling the flow of the water around my feet, and listening to its sounds, I really became part of the stream. Then I said a prayer to release my grief. I asked the waters to take it from me and carry it slowly downstream and out to sea. When ready, I turned around to face upstream and said a prayer to welcome in what I hoped for the next seven years and imagined all that possibility flowing towards me.

There was something about the water metaphorically washing, cleansing and replenishing me at a soul level that I found exquisite. And it helped ease my grief.

This exercise could be done standing on a bridge looking down at a river, or as a visualisation.

12

Being in the Moment

A change in life circumstance can have us reaching into the past or envisioning scenarios for the future. Neither of these scenarios are much help to us because life is what is happening in this moment now.

When we are faced with situations like months of medical treatment, or the unknowingness of moving to a new location, a new job, or other circumstances; keeping focused on *this moment now* helps prevent the tendency to take the whole projected experience on board. That load is too heavy and is the future, which, if we stop to think, is not where we are right now.

So this ability to *be in the moment* can help reduce overwhelm. It is powerful for self-care and wonderful for compassionate communication with others, helping them too to see that what matters, is this moment *now*.

Bringing focus down to the present moment allows us to see the shafts of sunlight that may be coming in through the window. Your pet may be looking at you with love in its eyes. You might notice a bird singing, or bush flowering. These things can helps us steady ourselves. This moment now can be *beautiful*. Being in the moment can help us show up for others when they need us most.

13

Finding a Safe Place to Land in the Middle of Things

I was first taught this very helpful technique many years ago at a crisis management training session in London.

Difficult conversations and moments in life can have the power to sweep us away. We can be overcome by emotion and circumstance. At the very moment when we need to be grounded and strong, we can feel anything but that. Yet, there is a simple technique we can use to keep things 'on an even keel'. I call it *finding a safe place to land in the middle of things*.

As an example of how to work with this idea, imagine having a conversation where we are hearing things that are painful to us, or speaking words that are difficult for the other. This approach encourages you to plan and think of an image or place you can return to in your mind that feels like a safe place to land. This could be the smile of a child, or a favourite tree, it could be a piece of music, or a stepping stone in a river. It could even be a phrase that you can repeat like "I am here to help".

When you start to feel overwhelm and you need time to formulate an answer, return to that safe place to land. Even for a second or two this can help you take a pause, find calm, find strength and stillness so you can then continue. Take a breath. Imagine the safe place, or gently speak your phrase, and then move forward from there.

14

Tapping to Help Relieve Anxiety

Tapping the body can help relieve anxiety. Here's why. The vagus nerve, or *wandering nerve*, is the longest cranial nerve in the body and is a part of the parasympathetic nervous system. It originates from the brain stem, runs through the neck and chest, and into your abdomen, branching off to different organs.

The vagus nerve is responsible for regulating the parasympathetic nervous system (PNS). The parasympathetic nervous system is responsible for restoring essential functions and soothing the body, like alleviating anxiety and reducing stress levels. While the sympathetic nervous system (SNS) is the system that responds to outside stimuli and is responsible for the fight or flight response.

The vagus nerve controls many body functions, such as heart rate, breathing, digestion, speaking, blood flow, and swallowing. It also plays a vital role in controlling emotions, but it can be affected by our response to things such as stress, fear etc.

If we tap lightly with our fingertips at the base of our throat and on our sternum (breastbone) we stimulate the vagus nerve, which then breaks the grip of the sympathetic nervous system's (SNS) 'fight or flight' response and in doing so, helps calm our system down.

Humming, or chanting sacred phrases like 'Om' have the same effect as tapping because they create a vibration in the chest.

15

Breathing into Pain

Whether emotional or physical, pain can be something that we want to run away from. Yet, breathing into pain can be a very effective helpful way of coping with, dissipating, or managing it. This may sound counter-intuitive, but it can be a highly effective way to help manage pain.

Take some moments to focus on your breathing with some slow and deep breaths.

Feel the sense of your physical form and then locate the pain within it. Where is the physical pain? Where is the emotional pain residing in your body? When you have it located, breath slowly into that place.

Imagine your breath comforting the pain, and each breath slowly but surely diminishing it.

16

What Really Matters

When a medical diagnosis starts changing everything, there can be a feeling of speed as appointments are navigated and treatment options planned. This rush and shock can bring with it a sense of losing sight of who one was before the diagnosis.

Care of the patient should care for the w*hole* of the person. That means their physical, emotional, intellectual and spiritual needs.

Wise healers through time have written that *"if the soul is ailing the body is sick."* These words are a gentle reminder that it is beneficial to find space to think about the things that matter beyond medical care. The things that nourish you at a soul level.

Holistic care is also about the things you love, the things that make a positive difference to your life such as music and art, the view from a window, being under a special tree in the garden, being at the beach, walking in the forest and the connections to family and friends. These are all *medicine for the soul.*

Find ways of connecting with the things that nourish and care for your soul, and this will help you navigate the rest of your medical journey.

17

Helping Those You Love Care for You

Help can be a strange thing. People want to help, but don't know how to, and we may feel embarrassed or compromised to ask for it. But it needn't be like this.

Write a list of all the things that would help you (or all the things you think you could do to help someone else).

It can help to think of it in different areas of your life like: practical things around the home, family care, pet care, creative wishes, spiritual care, dietary care.

Think about the things that need to be done, and the things that make a positive difference to your life. Then share this with family and friends so they can see the things that they may be able to help you with.

For example, there are only so many casseroles one can eat, but a drive to the beach one day would be incredible. Friends and family members could set up a roster to take turns helping a loved one out.

Never underestimate the desire to help. I've seen some great emails where someone has put down a whole list of things that could help them, from the mundane and practical to the big wish stuff like 'a holiday in Fiji'... and they got them all!

18

Paperwork for Peace of Mind

Unfortunately, illness or accident can strike at any time of life and because of this there are three pieces of paperwork that every adult should have in place, regardless of age because they make so much difference to caring for someone when they are suddenly no longer able to speak for themselves. These are:

-*Enduring Power of Attorney*. This is a legal document that gives someone the right to make decisions on your behalf when you can no longer speak for yourself.

There are two types and both needs attending to. One is for Health and Welfare i.e. decisions affecting your medical and life care; and Property, which relates to your finances and property decisions. You need to think carefully about who you want to make decisions for you. Often this is a partner or spouse but could also be a close friend.

The documents are signed by you both and validated by a lawyer. They only come into effect when you have been assessed as medically or mentally unfit to make decisions for yourself. Be sure to keep these documents up to date if relationships change, e.g. new partner.

- *Advance Care Plan.* This is not a legal document, but it gives directions regarding medical decisions you would want made on your behalf such as whether you want to be resuscitated, or feed via a feeding tube, or kept alive on life support or not.
- *Will.* This is a legal document that manages your affairs after you have died and enables you to state what property of yours goes to whom.

Make sure someone has a copy of these documents or knows where they are in the event they are needed. Without these documents no one can act on your behalf.

NB: In New Zealand, you can find the Enduring Power of Attorney and Will documents available online at The Public Trust *publictrust.co.nz*, or at your solicitor. Advance Care Planning information can be found at *health.govt.nz*

19

Finding a Place to Meet (even when absent)

Being geographically removed from someone you love; someone you want to be there for can be hard.

A technique that can be helpful for both of you is to say that at a certain time every day or week, you are going to stop everything you are doing and focus on that person. At that time, you will be sending them all your love and support and imagining yourself right there with them.

If you pray, then you could use this time to pray for them.

This need only take a minute or two, or longer if you wish, but its magic lies in both of you knowing this is happening at the same time, so you can both be conscious of this special connection at this time.

20

Transformational Power of an Altar

An altar is a designated place where you can direct energy and intention. It creates a sacred space in your home and a sacred connection to those you are caring for.

You can place things on the altar to represent the four elements of the universe: earth, air, fire and water. You might have a spiritual object like a cross or a buddha. And then you can place offerings on the altar like fresh flowers, a taonga, or a photo of someone you are thinking of.

You could use the altar to sit before to meditate or as your place to meet even when absent.

21

Aromatics as Medicine for The Soul

The Renaissance physician Marsilio Ficino (1433-1499) wrote at length about the use of aromatics as medicine for the spirit and soul. One of the prescriptions he would give his patients was to "walk at night in a scented garden". While he may have lived five hundred years ago, that advice is just as beautiful today as it was then.

What are the aromatics that nourish your soul?
What are the memories they conjure that you can enjoy returning to?

Put some drops of your favourite essential oil in an aroma diffuser and let its magic work. Or you could put a couple of drops on a tissue and inhale. You can find reputable essential oil suppliers easily available online. Be sure to purchase therapeutic grade and sustainably grown and harvested oils.

Some suggestions:

- Lavender essential oil has a calming effect;
- Vetiver has an earthy aroma and is known in India as *'the oil of tranquility'*;
- Geranium is said to have a balancing effect;
- Rosemary helps stimulate memory and focus;
- Cedar is very grounding;
- Frankincense has many spiritual associations.

Tip: do not purchase 'cosmetic grade' essential oils as they can be synthetic or cheaper plant extracts mixed to approximate the scent of the plant you thought you had bought.

22

The Asclepieion Temple of Dreams

In Ancient Greece, Asclepius was the God of Healing. Temples were made in his name to offer a special dream therapy called *incubatio*. People would come to the temple, fast for a few days and be taken to a special room where they would go to sleep on a bed, around which non-venomous Asclepieion snakes writhed on the floor. In many cultures, the snake represents our ability to shed and discard negativity in the same way they shed their skin, so their presence in the temple was seen as part of the healing and transformation that could take place. In the morning, a priest would come and listen to your dreams and then interpret them for you, helping you find the wisdom in their imagery.

Later in the 1500's, the Swiss physician and alchemist Paracelsus, wrote that the daytime is given to our physical being, but at night we have the power for our spirit to move upwards and join world spirit and tap into all knowledge of all time.

Asclepieion dream therapy and Paracelsus would encourage you to go to sleep with a question on your mind that you are seeking answers to or guidance with. They would encourage you to offer the question up to world spirit and in doing so, tap into all knowledge. This may be where the common phrase "I'll sleep on it" has come from.

Have a go at this yourself (maybe minus the snakes!). Then on waking write down any dreams you can remember and see if you can find the wisdom or insights you need.

23

Being the Tree

Being with Nature can be incredibly healing. It can help us feel less alone, more connected to life around us. It can be a place to find solace, release our burdens, renew our sense of vitality and spirit. In some cultures and traditions, trees are called Standing People. They don't move from their position, but they can see everything from all sides.

If we imagine ourselves as a tree, we can find roots to send down deep into the soil to help us feel grounded. Our trunk is tall and strong, it gives us strength. Its branches can contain so much life, a nesting bird, a spider's web.

The rustle of its leaves can be a song.

Higher up in those branches we can still feel the strength of our trunk and the grounding of our roots, but we have the flexibility to move with the winds. *This could be helpful to visualise when people are telling you different things and you're feeling overwhelmed - they shake your leaves but don't affect your strength.* And we also have vision. From up high in the top of the tree we can see everything above and below.

If we think like a tree, we can find the space to get above the problem and to see it from all sides. We can find stillness to reflect whole heartedly on a situation and then know just what to do.

24

Images as Amulets

Renaissance *'physician of the soul'* Marsilio Ficino, worked with the power of art, colour, music and object to draw down the powers of spirit and universe. He said that we should pay attention to the colours of our walls and the images we see around us because we will receive the energy of these images.

Ficino was saying that images can be part of your healing medicine. Images can extend to what we watch on our screens as well.

What are the images we are filling our senses with?

What is the energy they are transmitting?

If we start to think of images around us as amulets, what are the images you have around you that help you heal or find peace? What are the images that make you smile or relax you? What are the images that nourish your spiritual life?

Being conscious of the images we look at, thinking of them as amulets that contain a certain power, can make us become more selective about the things we wish to see because we better understand the effect they have upon us. We may choose to give more attention to images of loved ones, a painting that uplifts or creates a sense of tranquility, a restful colour on the wall.

There is much beauty to gaze upon in this world. And with it comes so much healing.

25

Communication Counts

Life changes are an invitation to deeper forms of communication. This invitation can deepen bonds between people. Communication can grow love even when you think it can't get any bigger than it is already.

The art of creating space for contemplation and conversation, using our ability to ask open questions and show up with no judgement can enhance our relationships with others in this moment right now. This is love and compassion working.

Why wait to be compassionate? Be it now.

26

Look Deep into Nature

The 16th Century physician and alchemist, Paracelsus, said, *"Nature is the universal teacher. Whatever we cannot learn from the external appearance of Nature we can learn from her spirit. Both are one. Nature is a light, and by looking at Nature in her own light we will understand her."*

Einstein echoed this with his own words, *"Look deep into Nature and you will understand everything better."*

When you are feeling stuck; when you are looking for guidance, or for a sign to help you in some way try looking for clues in Nature.

Taking time to be in Nature, not just superficially, but really giving yourself time and focus to deeply observe the natural world around you, will be deeply restorative and may help you find the insights and answers you are searching for.

27

The Empty Vessel

There are many descriptions in different spiritual texts that speak of earthenware vessels.

In my work with clients, I have found that guiding someone to envisage holding a beautiful earthenware vessel to their body can be powerful and comforting. They picture their arms around it. This earthly vessel is curved and generous in size. In hugging it, we are hugging the very clay of our being.

Within this earthen vessel we can picture our own divine essence and all the beauty and power of the universe. Holding it to our body, it becomes the universe embracing is. We can then imagine reaching into the vessel and gently pulling something out to explore further such as non-judgement, loving kindness, courage, release. We can also imagine the vessel full of cleansing waters and dropping something into it to be healed such as grief, fear, aloneness.

28

The Power of Thought

The 12th century mystic Hildegard of Bingen wrote extensively about the power of thought. She said that our own thoughts can create the world around us.

She explained that we are a microcosm of the macrocosm, or a universe within a universe. She described how the thoughts we have within us will be reflected to the world outside us and will create that world. *It's like when you think 'yellow car' and then all you keep seeing are yellow cars!*

What is the world we wish to create?

If we feel powerless, we will create a world around us in which we are powerless.

If we think of forgiveness, we will create a forgiving world.

If we are filled with thoughts of worry, anger or negativity for another person, the ancients would say that we are transmitting those emotions to that person.

Hildegard spoke of the idea of *'vices and virtues'* and the power of thought as a form of healing for the self, for others, and for the world.

She would encourage you to identify some negative messaging you tell yourself, for example "Bad things always happen to me" and she would call that the 'vice'. Then she would get you to think of the 'virtue' to replace it with. In this case it could be a phrase like "I am worthy of good fortune". Anytime the 'vice' phrase comes to mind, you call in the 'virtue' to replace it with. Focus on the virtue phrase, repeating it to yourself often.

In effect the things we tell ourselves can become a mantra. Words give us the power to reframe a situation or our sense of Self in the world, and in doing so, change the very world itself.

29

Counting Breaths I

There is much in this book about breath. Quite simply, *Breath is Life*. When we need to find calm amid the storm, breath can take us there.

A simple breath exercise is to count breath to create calm.

Breathe in for a count of four.
Hold your breath for a count of four.
Breathe out for a count of four.
Hold stillness for a count of four.

Sense the calm that starts to arise.

Do this exercise for as long and as often as needed.

30

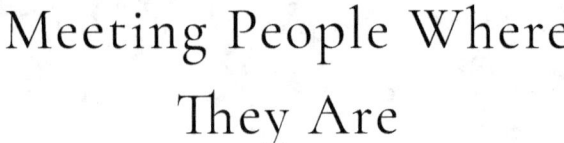

Meeting People Where They Are

Some years ago, I was in conversation with the truly inspirational author, psychotherapist and former monk, Thomas Moore, about the art of soulful conversation.

He said something that was so simple and so wise. He said, "*Meet people where they are. Don't try to take them to where you want to go.*"

We all have our own ideas of how a situation may unfold, but we only know our own reality, not the other person's.

When we are trying to support a loved one when life changes, we can't assume their reality. To truly help we need to truly understand where they are in this situation or moment in time. By asking open questions (No.8) and having the openness of *'don't know mind'* (No.3) we are better able to meet our loved one where they are. When meeting someone there, you have the possibility to move forward together.

31

Writing Letters for the Future

Frank Ostaseski, founder of the first Zen Hospice in the USA, has written a book called *The Five Invitations – discovering what death can teach us about living fully*. One of the invitations he writes about is *'Don't Wait'*.

We are so good at waiting. We say, 'One day I will do that thing'. But so often that one day never comes.

If there are things you want to tell someone you love one day, write a letter to them *now*, while this is on your mind. Write the things you want to tell a child at milestones of their life. Describe the gratitude you want to show a friend or a loved one. Record the stories you want to share, so that one day those you leave behind may understand you better. Write these stories now, for the future.

You could put them in envelopes addressed to that person and even with instructions as to when to open it (such as a graduation or wedding) and place the letters somewhere safe, with your other important paperwork (No.18) so that you get to say the things you want to say, when you want to say them. Imagine what a gift that will be for them when that time comes.

32

Finding Your Spirit Animal

We don't have to go through things on our own. We can call on others to help us, and this includes the animal world too. All cultures and traditions have attributed certain powers and characteristics to different animals, birds, reptiles, marine creatures, and insects and have worked with these powers in sacred ceremony and personal power.

Finding your *spirit animal* is an invitation to call on the animal whose powers you feel could benefit you, so that you can have them help you. You may wish to have the courage of a lion, or the peace of a dove, you may wish for the kingfisher's ability to move between worlds of the aquatic and the aerial. You may want to be like a snake and shed an old skin to move forward renewed. You may want the protection of a tiger, or the wisdom of an owl.

Working with the idea of identifying the animals that can be your spirit companions is empowering and transformational and can help you feel a little less alone.

What are the animals you are drawn to and what is it about them that you connect with or admire? What are their qualities that you could work with to help you navigate life?

33

Working with the Moon

Every 28 days the moon travels around Earth. Just as the tides are determined by its passage, so too we can work with its waxing and waning power for our own journey through life.

Each month has a pattern. The full moon will start to reveal less of itself, becoming a crescent and then a sliver. Then at New Moon it is not seen at all. This passage of disappearing is called *'waning'*.

After the New Moon, we start to see it again. A sliver, then a crescent and then the full illuminated moon. This passage of appearing is called *'waxing'*.

When the moon is *waning*, energy here on earth goes downwards. In the garden, the energy of plants retreats back to the earth. Energy goes inwards, it can be a time for introspection and withdrawal, or quietly knuckling down to the task at hand.

The darkness of New Moon is a pause, like the slack moment between tides. No movement. This is a good time to make plans and set intentions. Then as the moon *waxes*, energy and life force moves upwards and outwards. This movement can be used to bring ideas and plans to growth and fruition.

Learning to work with these rhythms can be beneficial as you can step into the flow of time itself.

34

The Power of Plant Essences

Plant essences, also known as flower remedies, are a form of vibrational medicine that help us deepen our relationship with nature and support our emotional life. They could be described as a way of connecting with the *life force* of a plant.

Plant essences are not aromatic extracts like essential oils. Where essential oils use large amounts of plant material to make very concentrated extracts, plant essences are made from small amounts of plant material and are capturing the energetics of that plant.

They help us create a quantum, energetic connection with plant allies, and provide a beautiful form of nature-based care. They do not affect other medicines and they support emotional wellbeing.

Plant essences help us tap into the qualities of a plant that can help us in our own lives. For example, the essence of rose may help us love ourselves more, or dandelion may help us better digest all that life puts in our path.

Plant essences can also be used to help bring people together in celebration, ritual, or remembrance. They can be added to drinks, food, hand bowls and used to sip, anoint, and diffuse. Plant essences are effective aids for meditation, yoga and other mind body practices and can be used by people of all ages as well as animals.

I have worked with plant essences in homes, workplaces, hospitals, hospices, care homes, churches, funeral homes and in nature and their effect has often been spellbinding.

35

The Power of Ceremony

The act of creating ceremony can make moments and transitions sacred. Even small, simple intentional moments can have profound power. Ceremony can create a pause in normal life, and enable us to step into a space that can be beautifully laden with meaning.

Ceremony is transformational and is enhanced by following a simple structure. A good ceremony has an intention, an opening, an offering, and something that enables the marking of the transformation being sought, and a closing. For example, a traditional wedding ceremony starts with people gathering. The bride walks up the aisle, the celebrant or minister then states the intention of being gathered together to witness the marriage. There may be offerings of prayers. The key moments of transformation are the vows, and the celebrant then marks the transformation by stating the couple are now man and wife. Then there is a closing song and blessing and the ceremony ends with the couple walking back down the aisle.

Recently I created an impromptu ceremony for three friends who had gathered on the anniversary of the death of one of their friends. I opened the ceremony by stating that they are gathered to remember their friend. Then I opened sacred space around them. I offered a blessing to them and their friend and invited them to have a moment's silence to send their own thoughts and prayers to their friend. The moment of transformation was when each person anointed themselves with a drop of rosemary plant essence for remembrance, and then anointed the other two present. This was a profound part of the ceremony, creating deep connection between the friends and a beautiful way of honouring their friend. I then closed the ceremony with a blessing and closed the sacred space.

A ceremony can be as simple as lighting a candle and sending a prayer to someone you love. We are only limited by imagination. Examples of situations that can be enhanced by ceremony include, leaving a house, entering a new relationship, acknowledging a divorce, honouring an intent to start a new practice, remembering a friend who has died, showing gratitude for the healing power of a landscape, seeing a child leave home for university, honouring the completion of a project, blessing family bonds in times of change.

What is something in your life that you could honour or transform with a ceremony, and how might you create it?

36

Counting Breath II

There are times when we can help another to calm their breathing. In times of great fear and anxiety, or during a transition into new life stages such as birthing into life or death, counting breath is lifted beyond the mundane into a sacred act. In these times we become midwives of the soul.

I finally truly understood this when I was at my father's side for the last few days of his life. His breath was racing, and he was anxious. I held his hand and started to slow my own breathing, quietly and audibly counting my breath to a beat of four (No.29). He looked at me and started to try to follow my breath. He started to grow calmer. His breathing slowed. Not as slow as mine, but slower than before. I felt him squeeze my hand.

In that moment, I thought of all the midwives helping mothers breathe into their birthing pains, and here I was helping midwife my father, helping him breathe into the labour pains of his own final transition.

Whenever I recall those moments, when I see myself back at the bedside, counting slow beats to four, I am filled with a huge and profound love.

37

Handing Back the Wounds that are Not Yours to Carry

Shamanism speaks of intergenerational wounds - the attitudes, fears, self-limiting stories that a parent may unwittingly hand to their child, on and on down through time.

But we don't have to carry these wounds, and we don't have to hand them down to the next generation.

Life changes and challenging transitions can bring these stories to the fore. But rather than let them dominate your response to events, you could free yourself from them.

Find a quiet place to think about your parents' stories, or the stories of your ancestors, and think about or write down the things you can see that have held them back, or have become the thing that they, or the family at large, define themselves by, good and bad. Then separate the good things from the bad.

Create a sense of sacred space and ceremony (No.35) and imagine yourself saying to family and ancestors that these wounds are not yours to carry and that you are releasing them from the family line.

You could write each wound or story on a separate piece of paper and then ceremonially place the paper into a fire to release it from the family line.

Then take the positive attributes you see running through your family and one by one, thank your family and ancestors for these gifts and ask for their blessing so you may use these gifts well.

This process can be incredibly healing for all involved.

38

A Blessing for Your Body

If life is changing due to illness or infirmity, we can find ourselves directing a lot of anger at our body. Why is it failing us? But the power of thought is powerful medicine (No.28) and so taking time to remember that it was not always this way can be a beautiful help to resetting the changing relationship with one's body.

This technique can be done alone or with loved ones like a partner or children. Light a candle to represent your soul and its eternal nature. Then slowly work through your body thanking it for the experiences it has given you to date.

This can also be done for someone. For example, if someone is very ill, this could be done as a blessing by loved ones to them.

For example:

"I thank my brain for all the knowledge and creativity it has given me"
"I thank my eyes for letting me see so much beauty, like the beauty of you my partner, or the beauty of you my child"
"I thank my lips for all the kisses they have given to those I love"
"I thank my tongue for all the delicious tastes I have experienced"
"I thank my fingers for all that they have gripped and touched."
"I thank my legs and feet for all the places they have helped me travel."

39

Holding Healing Space

Sometimes the most useful and caring thing we can do for someone is to hold healing space for them. This can be done by anyone. We first invite everyone present to focus on their breath. We invite them to feel themselves deepening their connection to the earth, and to also imagine a chord coming up through the crown of their head and connecting them to the universe.

Invite them to place their hands in prayer position in front of their heart, and then slowly move their hands pressed together above their head. Once above their head, turn the hands back-to-back and imagine sweeping down a golden light, like an orb around them, and then around each other. If they are unable to follow the movements, your own actions are creating the space for all. You can repeat this sweeping movement as many times as you like until you feel that you have created this beautiful orb around you all. You could also extend it over your home, community or even the world.

When you feel settled, thank the helping spirits and energies that are there to support you all. You could ask them to hold your loved one in their loving care. You have created a healing space. When your session is drawing to a close, thank the helping spirits again and imagine rolling the orb back up (almost like the sides of a tent) and returning it to the universe.

I remember some years ago, sitting with someone who was in pain and nearing death, and I created and held sacred space for them. I felt the room filling up with gentle healing light. It was spacious and timeless. Then at the exact moment I felt a bolt of energy go through me, the person said out loud, "I feel so cared for now".

40

Talking to Children

Never underestimate the wisdom and awareness of a child. We will never have all the information we wish for to prepare ourselves for talking to children about changes in health or circumstance. We can often avoid talking to them about a situation because we don't want to worry or upset. In the case of illness, children will cope more effectively when they know what is happening and, within their cognitive abilities, what to expect.

Let them ask questions. Know that it is OK to not have all the answers. Ways to help them ask questions could be to have a noticeboard that they can write questions on as they come to mind or have a 'talking shell' or object that they can pick up and show you when they have a question on their mind. You could set aside a regular time for family members to come together to talk about things.

Include them in navigating this new phase of life. See them for the individual they are and help them find ways to show up for others too. Many people say that once they talked to the children a load of stress was taken off their shoulders and it strengthened connections within the family unit.

Here are some tips from the Cancer Society NZ, but this advice extends beyond illness into other life changes too:

At first, you may want to talk to children individually. They may need to know different things because of age or development level. Later, it might be comfortable for you to talk about some things together as a family. You may want to practice what you will say and anticipate what questions your children might ask. You will want to talk in a language each child understands - some children understand more when you draw pictures, use books, or both. Assure them they will still be loved and cared for.

Listen to them. Let them know it is okay to ask questions. Answer their questions simply. Ask them if they have understood your answers.

41

Speaking Silently Through the Heart

You can work with energetic intent to connect, communicate and comfort loved ones.

Imagine sending them loving kindness and compassion, like a pulse of pure light from your heart to their heart. As you do this ask for the highest benefit of healing for that person and to all. Picture sending love directly from your heart into the heart of the person.

Speak silently to their heart, affirming their life and all your connections to each other. You could also envisage them in a setting they love like a place in nature, or their home, creative environment etc., and beam that image to them.

You'll find that this process can also help lift some of the feeling of helplessness from your shoulders.

42

I Am Still Standing

Part of caring for others is caring for ourselves.
Be kind to yourself.
Your inner and outer worlds need looking after too.

43

Bringing Nature into the Room

When a loved one is ill in bed, moving through an illness, recuperating after treatment, restricted by failing mobility, nearing the end of life, the natural world can start to become very distant. Yet perhaps this person used to love to walk in the forest, feel the sand under their feet by the ocean, enjoy the feeling of their hands in the soil in their garden, ride their horse across the hills. Now they are unable to get out into nature, but they are still that person.

So how can you bring nature to them?
What are the landscapes and places in nature they loved?
What are their favourite flowers? What smells do they like?

You have the power to bring many of their connections with nature into the room. You could do it through the images (No.24) you place in the room where they can see them. You could work with aromatics (No.21). You could put fresh flowers in a vase, open a window so they can hear the birds. You could play the sound of bird calls or other animals they love. You could use your own imagination to create the landscape for them with words (no. 44).

44

Creating Guided Visualisations

The imagination is a powerful tool of creation and healing, and when used to create guided meditations and visualisations for a loved one, magic can happen.

In effect, this work is a form of storytelling. You are creating a world with your words.

You could create a visualisation that helps them prepare for a hospital visit, creating a scenario where they are cared for and an added divine force is working for them during their treatment or intervention.

Maybe they are in bed recuperating, and you could slowly guide them through a story of their own healing.

Perhaps they are unable to go outside and so you can take them to their favourite landscape with the simple power of your words.

I have used this technique in so many ways and each time have seen how extraordinarily powerful and loving it can be.

If approached with a sense of *meeting the person where they are* (No.30) and asking them what they would wish to be experiencing in this moment now, great care and resonance can be created.

45

Everything is Energy (how we show up for others)

Communication takes many forms and what is said without words can be even more impactful than the things we speak, because energy travels and we pick up on it, and when someone is unwell this ability to pick up on the energy in the room can become even more acute.

If we rush into the room of a loved one who is not well, they will feel our rushed energy. If we are angry or scared, heartbroken or frustrated, they will feel that too. Conversely, if we enter the room with calming, loving energy this will be what is felt by the others present.

A technique that can help to manage one's emotions can be to envisage your auric field, or light body. This is the energetic 'bubble' that surrounds you.

Imagine filling that bubble with loving kindness and compassion. Imagine filling it with calm, or confidence. And when you think you have filled it to the brim with love, just add a little bit more. Then when you come into connection with others, this bubble of love is what they will sense. You can consciously hold the image of this bubble, keeping it full and kind. And after a while not only you will feel it working on the person you are with, but also on your state of being too.

46

Don't Be Afraid of Silence

Sometimes your loving presence is all that is needed in this moment.

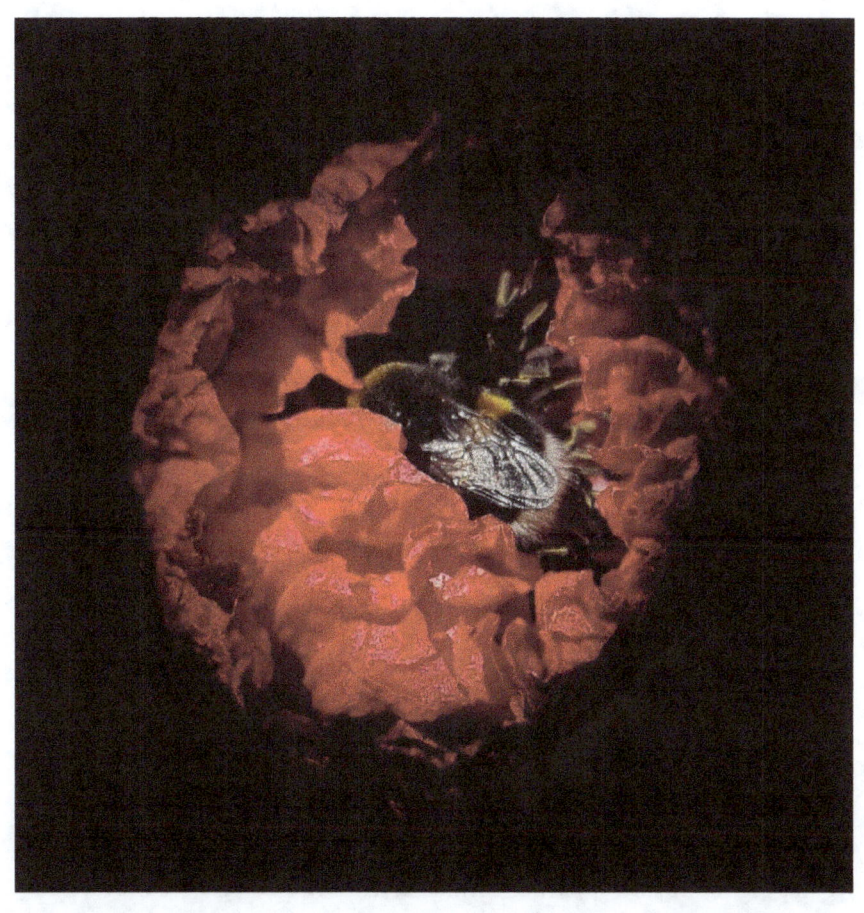

47

Written in the Sky

Hippocrates, the ancient Greek philosopher, and father of modern medicine said, *"to be a physician, first you must know the stars"*.

There is something beautiful about looking up at the night sky at the end of the day, or in the early morning before dawn.

An ancient and symbolic word for the universe is *cosmos*. The meaning of cosmos is *"a well ordered and harmonious universe which contains everything needed for life."* In the days before Netflix and streetlights, the ancients looked up into the inky night and saw us written large across that starlit sky. They said we were a *microcosm of the macrocosm*, in other words, a *universe within a universe*. They saw our health and wellbeing in the context of our relationship to Nature, spirit, and cosmos. The movement of planets through constellations became laden with meaning as well as symbolic and spiritual connections to life down here on earth.

Even a few moments of time gazing up at the night sky can help create a sense of calm and wonder. And, if city lights interfere with your view of the night sky, there are apps that can show us the exact position of planets and stars in relation to where we are standing.

Seeing ourselves as part of something so beautifully vast has a poetry to it. We can look up and sense that we are connected to all that we see: stars, planets, the moon, the earth beneath our feet.... everything is connected. We are, as philosophers of old would say, quite literally *"made of stardust"*.

There is much healing in that idea.

48

Don't Hold Back, Experience Everything

There is so much joy in the phrase *don't hold back, experience everything*. I first read it in Frank Ostaseski's book *The Five Invitations*. The more I have worked with the dying, the more I think about the richness of this phrase. None of us like to think about death, but the paradox is that when we recognise it as a natural part of life, it can make the living of life even more of a treasure. Diagnosis of a life-limiting condition can be a shock. It makes us see that death will happen, but also it can invite us to recognise that each moment of life is precious, *so let us live it. Let us not hold back, let's experience everything.*

Death can teach us so much about living. Seeing death as a natural part of the life cycle can give us a sense of deep gratitude in for the time we have in our body, with its powers to enable a sensory and emotional connection with the world, With these connections, we have the power to live as fully as we can alone, and in community with others. Don't wait. If you want to tell someone you love them, *tell them you love them*. If you want to jump in puddles or hug your child one more time.... don't hold back, *do it*. Experience everything.

49

Fire as a Tool for Transformation

Fire is a tool for transformation. Lighting a candle can be a sacred, soulful act.

In the ancient Hindu tradition, the soul or *agni*, is believed to be a flame flickering in the heart space.

A candle can be lit in celebration, in memory or in meditation. A candle can symbolise the bringing in of light, or the fading of the light.

Writing fears and things we wish to let go of onto a piece of paper and then putting it into a fire can help release burdens.

50

In the End Love is All There Is

In 1833 Lord Alfred Tennyson write, *"Tis better to have loved and lost than never have loved at all."*

When life changes, relationships end, children leave the nest, an illness consumes someone we love, or consumes ourselves... love is the greatest gift.

We know that death comes to all of us. We know that like the seasons there is a time for beginnings and a time for endings.

We know that great grief grows from great love, but love can help heal this all.

Love is that strange ephemeral thing that we feel with our whole self. It can bring us so much joy and so much pain, but to imagine a life without it, that is pain indeed.

About the Author

Georgina Langdale is an ecotherapist, life transition guide, artist and author, and founder of the Archeus Apothecary. She helps people nurture their emotional, physical, creative and spiritual needs in life, and at the end of life. Her practice is deeply rooted in our connections to nature, and weaves together herbalism, compassionate and contemplative care, ecotherapy and spiritual accompaniment. She offers coaching, courses, workshops and products.

Her professional development includes training as a Sacred Passage Doula and Coach with the Conscious Dying Institute, IWHI Menopause coach, Reiki master, Four Winds Shamanic Energy Medicine graduate. She is a member of OBOD, the Climate Coaching Alliance, International End of Life Doula Association INELDA and the International Coaching Federation.

In 2013, Georgina established Archeus, an intentional artisanal apothecary specializing in crafting premium, natural products to support wellbeing through life transitions. Before founding Archeus, Georgina worked for the Royal Botanic Gardens Kew, the UN Environment Programme and in the arts and media. In 2024 Georgina will be ordained as an Interfaith Minister with the Onespirit Interfaith Foundation UK.

Georgina lives in New Zealand, with her husband Al and dog Bonnie.

Acknowledgments

I want to give thanks to my teachers and mentors who have helped me on my contemplative journey. These include Thomas Moore, A.T. Mann, the Conscious Dying Collective, OneSpirit Interfaith Foundation, Dale Borglum, Frank Ostaseski, Joan Halifax, Alberto Villoldo, Sandra Ingerman, Shu Shimaoka.

I want to thank Hildegard of Bingen, Marsilio Ficino, Paracelsus, Meister Eckhart, Rumi, Ptolemy, Buddha and the many other visionaries and mystics of old who have reached down through time to touch me and inspire me so profoundly. The greatest teachers of all have been Nature, and the many people I have walked with as they navigated their own life changes and transitions.

My thoughts and love I give to Sam, Sophie, Tāne, Manaia, Milo, Harry, Kate, Matt, Tom, Joe, Zoe, Alice, John, Ramona, Arlo, John, Karin, Evelyn, Theo, Robyn, Rob, to my husband Al, and all those who love all of these beautiful people.

Georgina

Helpful Links & Information

Georgina Langdale (coaching, mentorship, workshops, plant essences, compassionate care products, aromatics)
georginalangdale.com
Instagram @georginalangdalesoul
Youtube @archeusgeorgina
Podcast: The Soul Garden

Thomas Moore
thomasmooresoul.com

Frank Ostaseski
mettainstitute.org

Dale Borglum
livingdying.org

Cancer Society NZ
cancer.org.nz

Public Trust
publictrust.co.nz

Notes On Images

I didn't want captions to be a distraction within the pages of the book, as I wanted 'clear space' for your own interpretation. But I thought it might be nice to share a little about each of the images here.

Pg.7 Meadowsweet (Filipendula ulmaria) has deep significance for me. It is a common woodland plant in the UK and has a multitude of medicinal uses. Its scent is honey sweet. I planted some in my garden in New Zealand to create a link to my British Isles heritage and earth-based practices.

Pg.9 Silver Birch (Betula alba) is known by some as a deep protective female spirit and which has earned it the name of 'Lady of the Woods'. This tree was part of a birch glade growing at our last property and has watched over many blessings and healing work.

Pg.11 I took this photo of poppies growing in my medicine wheel garden in front of my studio and apothecary. It was late afternoon, and the water sprinkler was going. I just love the dreamy quality of this image.

Pg.13 These Hollyhocks (Rosea althea) were growing by my apothecary. I had gathered the seeds from plants growing in my mother's garden.

Pg.15 I took this photo while staying at Eibingen Abbey, in Germany, which was founded by Hildegard of Bingen in the 12th Century.

Pg.19 Hawthorn is used in herbal medicine as a heart remedy. I love to make plant essences with it to work with emotional issues related to the heart. I love it because it has such a calming and balancing energy.

Pg.25 This majestic oak tree is in a wood in England where I scattered some of my father's ashes.

Pg.27 This is a Roman ford in a stream in Wiltshire. The stones were covered in moss and the greenness of the trees and the dappled light on the water made this place quite magical.

Pg.29   These Echinacea (Echinacea purpurea) are growing in my garden, and I adore them. In herbal medicine they are used to help fight acute infections. I like making plant essences with them to work energetically to protect from negative influences.

Pg.35   Motherwort (Leonurus cardiaca) is an archetype plant for women, especially in midlife and beyond. Her botanical name means 'lionhearted' and I love working with her to support women through the menopause transition.

Pg.37   This passage leads from the guest rooms at Eibingen Abbey to the chapel. I took this photo as I made my way to Terce prayers at dawn. Magical.

Pg.39   Ocean Beach in Hawke's Bay, New Zealand is our nearest beach to where my husband and I live. It never fails to offer breathtaking views.

Pg.43   These hills are in Wiltshire near Kingston Deverill and they seemed to glow in the summer light.

Pg.45   This dear little altar is in my garden.

Pg.51   This majestic Totara tree is in Otari, Wilton's Bush in Wellington, New Zealand.

Pg.53   One of the ultimate amulets – Stonehenge, in England.

Pg.55   I carved this figure from pumice stone many years ago. I love how the moss has gathered on her over the years.

Pg.57   This creek is on the farm I grew up on in New Zealand. This spot was one of my mother's favourite places, and I buried her ashes by the bank here. It is a place I return to often as it is so peaceful and sacred.

Pg.59   This is the first ceramic pot I ever bought. I was a teenager and I found it in Russell, in the Bay of Islands in New Zealand. Sadly, I don't know the name of the potter. I adore ceramics and have gone on to collect works from around the world.

Pg.63   This thoughtful terracotta figure is in my garden. I call her 'The Herbalist', and she is made by Hawke's Bay artist, Kay Bazzard.

Pg.65   This statue was in the garden of a property we used to live at. I love the autumn colours in this image.

Pg.67   Speaking of autumn, I love these autumn leaves.

Pg.69   Our dog Bonnie just loves walks in this local reserve.

Pg.71   Full moon from the garden.

Pg.77   This is another figure by the wonderfully talented local artist Kay Bazzard. I call him Ficino, and he watches over my studio and apothecary.

Pg.87   Love in the Mist (Nigella sativa) is such a stunningly beautiful plant and is throughout my garden. It is an important medicinal herb in ayurvedic and Arabic traditions. I collect the seeds to use in cooking, and I make plant essences from the flowers.

Pg.89   The Rollright Stones in Oxfordshire is a neolithic stone circle and a favourite spot of mine.

Pg.91   The green plant in the foreground of this image is plantain (Plantago major) growing in my garden. Plantain has many healing qualities and I use it in a multitude of ways from teas, to balms. It was also one of the 12th century mystic Hildegard of Bingen's favourite healing herbs.

Pg.93   I spent almost a whole day watching and waiting for this monarch butterfly to eclose. It was most definitely worth the wait. A magical thing to witness.

Pg.95   A beautiful little Strawflower (Xerochrysum bracteantha) in my garden. They are also known as Everlasting or Immortelle.

Pg.97   This gorgeous bumblebee was deep within a poppy in the garden.

Pg.101   This sign is by a path through a reserve near where we live and each time I pass it I smile as its invitation to experience everything is irresistible.

Pg. 103   Who doesn't love the romantic waft of smoke after you blow a candle out?

Pg.105   This is a photo of my beloved dog Puffle. Sometimes you get lucky enough to have a very special animal arrive in your life, and for me Puffle was that animal. She died in 2022 and I miss her every day.

About Archeus Publishing

Archeus Publishing is a division of Archeus and launched in 2024 to publish books, audiobooks and recordings on ecotherapy, end of life care, spirituality, meditation and ancient wisdom.

Archeus Publishing
PO Box 8759
Havelock North 4130
New Zealand